Bible Study Series

Book 1: Relationships

By: Nicole Homan

Blessed is the man
who walks not in the counsel of the wicked,
nor stands in the way of sinners,
nor sits in the seat of scoffers;
² but his delight is in the law of the Lord,
and on his law he meditates day and night.

³ He is like a tree
planted *by streams of water*
that yields its fruit in its season,
and its leaf does not wither.
In all that he does, he prospers.

Psalm 1:1-3, ESV

Hello, friend!

The Planted Bible Study Series is designed to help you dig into Scripture and apply the truth of His Word to your everyday life. The topics were chosen prayerfully. As a mom of fourteen children, I have found the words of Psalm 1 to be true. As I "plant" myself in the Word of God, I become like the tree that is planted by streams of living water – yielding fruit, full of life, and prospering in all I do. And when I don't, I can feel myself dry up. My strength withers. My joy fades. My peace disappears. I become the mom I don't want to be – the one that is irritable, ungracious, and grumpy.

These Studies are unedited notes taken directly from my journals. They are lessons that God has taught me over the years. Some have not been easy, but all have been worth it. God's Word has changed my life and I know it will change yours too!

For more information about the ministry of Planted, go to our website: www.plantedministry.com.

Pursuing Jesus,

Nicole

Founders of Planted Ministry

Part 1

Start in the Garden

Lesson 1

"In the beginning, God created (Genesis 1:1)…" As I read the story of creation found in Genesis 1 & 2, I often find myself trying to imagine what it must have been like to watch beams of light birth and expand at the sound of God's voice; to watch nothing become something as He spoke. I close my eyes and picture the movement of the water as land came to the surface. I listen for the call of the newly-formed birds flying overhead. I attempt to envision the reaction of heaven as the angels watched Creator God breathe out stars (Psalm 33:6). And as I do, I find myself so overwhelmed by the One *"who spoke and it came to be* (Psalm 33:9)."

Genesis 1:26-27

"²⁶ Then God said, "Let us make man in our image, after our likeness. And let them have dominion over the fish of the sea and over the birds of the heavens and over the livestock and over all the earth and over every creeping thing that creeps on the earth."

²⁷ So God created man in his own image,
in the image of God he created him;
male and female he created them."

Genesis 1:31 says that *"God saw everything that he had made, and behold, it was very good."* It was "very good." Not bad. Not a mistake. Not an accident. Not an "oops." All that He had made – sky, mountain, ocean, animal – all of it was good. As an artist, I am captured by this statement. So often I have looked back upon a song I wrote, a picture I painted, or a poem I penned and thought, "It's okay, but I should have probably done this instead."

I always see the areas of weakness - the smudges of the paint, the lyrical moment I missed, and the rhyme that doesn't sit as perfectly in the phrase. Because of this, it's hard for me to fathom the moment when Creator God leaned back upon His throne and took in the entirety of what He had made and saw no flaw in it. To perfectly pour your vision unto the canvas and step back to see it's exactly what you had hoped for? No wonder David's Psalms speak so often of creation singing God's praise. How could it not? In Psalm 139 verse 14, David joins in declaring, *"I will praise you (God) for I am fearfully and wonderfully made."* **No other response but praise exists when faced with the reality of all that He has made.** Truly *"marvelous"* are His works!

- In your own words, describe the world that God had created:

- Look up the word "Good" in a dictionary or Strong's Concordance. What does the word mean? Write the definition below:

- Do you think this word could still be used to define our world? Why or why not?

Now, let's read **Genesis 2:18-25** and continue the story.

"¹⁸ Then the L<small>ORD</small> God said, "It is not good that the man should be alone; I will make him a helper fit for him." ¹⁹ Now out of the ground the L<small>ORD</small> God had formed every beast of the field and every bird of the heavens and brought them to the man to see what he would call them. And whatever the man called every living creature, that was its name. ²⁰ The man gave names to all livestock and to the birds of the heavens and to every beast of the field. But for Adam[c] there was not found a helper fit for him. ²¹ So the L<small>ORD</small> God caused a deep sleep to fall upon the man, and while he slept took one of his ribs and closed up its place with flesh. ²² And the rib that the L<small>ORD</small> God had taken from the man he made[d] into a woman and brought her to the man. ²³ Then the man said, "This at last is bone of my bones and flesh of my flesh; she shall be called Woman, because she was taken out of Man."

²⁴ Therefore a man shall leave his father and his mother and hold fast to his wife, and they shall become one flesh. ²⁵ And the man and his wife were both naked and were not ashamed."

As God took in the beauty of all that He had created, He saw that it wasn't good for Adam to be alone.

- Go back to your definition of "good" on the previous page. When God said that is was not good for Adam to be alone, what did He mean?

What Adam was lacking in his loneliness was something that would make his life better. God knew that relationship would add value to Adam's life and, because of this, God created Eve – a help mate and a companion.

- Have you ever felt lonely? Or isolated?

- Did that isolation or loneliness affect you? How?

- Why do you think God felt it wasn't good for Adam to be alone? Why do you think God felt Adam needed relationship?

We live in a world full of distractions, busy schedules, screens, alarms, calendars, check lists, commitments – a world that too often pulls us away from relationship. **We say, "I'll get to it," but, too often, we aren't.** Marriages are crumbling. Real intimacy is being traded in for momentary satisfaction from a computer screen. Couples who don't know how to fight have stopped fighting altogether. Friendships feel more like an inconvenience than a blessing. People wound each other through words slung from computer keyboards instead of mouths. Co-workers are simply that – co-workers. Not friends. Families aren't talking. Screens are drawing our gazes away from faces. Churches are emptying because of offense. The statistics are staggering. And I wonder how God's heart must feel as He watches it all unfold? This was not His plan. The God who looked down upon Adam and acknowledged, "*It is not good for man to be alone…,*" created relationship for a reason.

People of God, we need each other.

Psalm 68:5-6

> *"Father of the fatherless and protector of widows*
> *is God in his holy habitation.*
> *[6] God settles the solitary in a home;*
> *he leads out the prisoners to prosperity,*
> *but the rebellious dwell in a parched land."*

He put the "one" into the "many" for a reason.

Ecclesiastes 4:12

"¹² And though a man might prevail against one who is alone, two will withstand him—a threefold cord is not quickly broken."

Take a pencil in your hand. Break it. See how easily it bends? Now, grab a handful of pencils. Bear down on them with all of your might. Can you break them? If you are anything like me – you can't. Why? Because, like us, pencils are stronger together.

Animals know this. It's why prey like Zebras and Caribou travel in herds across the Savannah. Together they stand a chance. Alone they are a sitting target.

- Is there a relationship in your life that has made you feel stronger when facing a challenge? How?

Proverbs 27:17 says that like *"iron sharpens iron,"* so a man sharpens his friend. I have always questioned what was meant by this statement. That was until my children and I studied the medieval times and the work of a blacksmith. As I read from our history books of the blacksmith's hammer pounding upon the sword to make it sharp, I began to realize the depth of what was being said. As the blacksmith worked, sparks flew. There was friction, pounding, crashing, clashing, and heat. Out of that came the sharpening. In our lives we have "encouragers" and "challengers." Relationships that are hard and challenging God is using to grow us, teach us, and make us more like Him. The reality is this: **I can't be who God wants me to be without you**. This isn't just about my happiness. Relationships are the "tool" that God often uses to make us to make us holy.

- Do you see how God is using your relationships to grow you and stretch you?

- List some of the ways you have grown to be more like Jesus because of the relationships in your life:

Read these last two portions of scripture and write down the reasons they share with us as to why relationships matter:

Ephesians 4:16, 2:22

Psalm 133

When we all come together in unity, we will see His glory, His blessing, and His anointing released.

Genesis 3:8 tell us that *"they (Adam and Eve) heard the sound of the Lord God walking in the garden in the cool of the day…"* In the Garden of Eden not only did God establish man's relationship with on another, He also established a relationship between man and Himself. As evening settled upon the Garden, He came close to walk with them. He called them each by name. He didn't create them and disappear. He didn't rule them from a distance. He was present, engaged, and near. In this, we find an important truth that we each must grab ahold of: **God**

wants and has always wanted a relationship with His children.

1 John 3:1

"What manner of love is this that we should be called the children of God?"

Romans 5:8

"But God demonstrated His love for us in this – while we were yet sinners, Christ died for us."

All throughout scripture we see a God who:

1. Welcomes home prodigals (Luke 15).
2. Forgives the unforgiveable (John 8).
3. Gives second, third, and fiftieth chances (Malachi 3).
4. Carries the weak upon his shoulders (Luke 15).
5. Promises to reveal Himself to those who seek Him (Proverbs 8:17).
6. Willingly paid the price to "reconcile" us when we had broken the relationship (Romans 5).
7. And speaks to His people (Exodus 33).

He isn't distant. He isn't far off. From the Garden, He has been calling His children by name and drawing us to Himself with "*chords of loving-kindness* (Hosea 11:4)."

Let's finish **Genesis 3:8**.

"...And the man and his wife hid themselves from the presence of the Lord God among the trees of the garden."

- What did Adam and Eve do when God called to them?

- Read verses 1-7 leading up to this portion of scripture. Why do you think they responded to His call this way?

- Do you still think that people hide from relationship? Why or why not?

- Do you still think that fear plays a role in how close we get to others? If so, how?

Adam and Eve's sin breaks the connection between God and man. Isaiah 59:2 tells us that sin builds a "*barrier*." The result? Their connection with one another suffers. And it's here we find another important truth to grab ahold of: **Our relationships with others will always be affected by our relationship with God.** We cannot neglect it.

The moment Adam and Eve built a "barrier" between them and God, things changed. Continue the story and you will find Adam's first born son killing their younger son in a jealous rage, division, broken relationships, isolation, and family strife – all of this, a result of sin. Never was it God's plan. Never was it God's heart for mankind. Sin did this. Sin always does this – divides, destroys, devastates…and ultimately leads to death. Nothing good comes from it. Nothing good will ever come from it.

Open your Bible and let's read **2 Corinthians 5:18-19.** Underline it if you are comfortable. Take a moment and sit with the words written within this letter to Corinth. Lay hold of the depths of love that would motivate God to give His only begotten son to reconcile us to Him; to restore the relationship and connection destroyed because of man's sin, not His. In this we see yet another important truth: **God STILL desires relationship with His children.**

Look up the following portions of scripture and write down what they tell us about our relationship with God:

Revelation 3:20

John 15:15

- Do you feel that God is your "friend?" How would you describe your relationship with God?

- On an average week, how much time do you spend in the Word and in prayer?

- Do you see the connection between your closeness to God and the depth of your relationships with others? If yes, explain.

- When you look over the past weeks, do you see your relationship with God as something you "fit in" or as something you prioritize?

Years ago I asked women to share with me what relationship in their lives had suffered the most since becoming mothers. The list was simple: God, Spouse, Friendship, Family Relationships, and Church Family. The results shook me to my core. 99% of the women polled said that the number one relationship that had suffered the most since their children arrived was their relationship with God.

People of God, this can't be.

If there is any hope for our marriages, our families, and our friendships – it's found in Him and Him alone. He is the answer. His wisdom, His truth, His strength – we need it all. If we are going to have any chance of walking in close relationship with those around us, it starts with securing our relationship with God. It can't just be something we "fit in." It has to become a priority.

Application Questions

1. What relationships in my life needs to be my focus over the next few weeks?

2. What will I do this week to intentionally cultivate deeper connections with these people in my life?

3. What is my biggest "take-a-way" from this lesson?

4. What can I take off my plate to make time to invest in my relationships? Are there some more ways that I can invest in my relationship with God this week?

Lesson 2

Let's begin in **Psalm 139:13-16.**

"¹³ For you formed my inward parts;
you knitted me together in my mother's womb.
¹⁴ I praise you, for I am fearfully and wonderfully made.
Wonderful are your works;
my soul knows it very well.
¹⁵ My frame was not hidden from you,
when I was being made in secret,
intricately woven in the depths of the earth.
¹⁶ Your eyes saw my unformed substance;
in your book were written, every one of them,
the days that were formed for me,
when as yet there was none of them."

I read this and realize that not one detail of who I am – who you are - is a mistake. Not one of my thousands of freckles is out of place. We are "wonderful" – distinct and rare, one of a kind, extraordinary and special. Not an accident, not a failed-attempt – we are His masterpiece.

In fact, **Ephesians 2:10** calls us "God's workmanship" which is translated in the Jewish Bible as "work of art."

That is what I am…and what you are.

Vincent Van Gogh's Starry Night and Da Vinci's Mona Lisa all rolled into one and then some. God's Sistine Chapel. But too often, we can't see it. I always thought insecurity was the struggle of women. After pastoring for over a decade, I have come to discover that Satan doesn't care who you are. Men and women of God must root themselves deeply into the truth of their identity in Christ, because the enemy lies to all of us.

Let's open up God's Word and read **Genesis 3:1-7** again.
- Who is speaking to Eve in this portion of scripture?

- What picture does the serpent paint of God when talking to Eve?

- Does the picture He paints of God match what we know of God from lesson 1 – a God who is good and who wants relationship with His children?

The Devil says, **"If you….then you…"** And as I read these words, I realize this same lie is being sold on television screens and magazine racks today.

If you wear this size of clothing, then you will be the right size.

If you lost ten pounds, then you will feel pretty.

If you weren't so tall, short, scrawny, fat, dumb, annoying - then others would like you.

If you make six figures, then you will be valuable.

If you get the trophy, then you will be worthwhile.

If you had more muscles, then she would notice you.

It's everywhere. The media constantly bombards us with ads about products that will "fix us" or "make us better."

Bald? *There is a product for that!*

Too short? *Here are some shoe lifts!*

Too tall? *Here is a way you can style your hair to look shorter!*

Crooked nose? *I have the name of a great plastic surgeon!*

Need more muscles? *Here's a shirt that makes you look ripped!*

Don't fit in at work? *Let me share with you my five easy steps to popularity. Step 1: Get a new personality!*

With all of this, it can be hard not to feel like Eve and give in to the lie.

When I was in High School, movie after movie came out about girls who were labeled "nerds" or "losers" that would be made over and turned into prom queens. The popular guy would inevitably melt at their feet and fall madly in love with them, but only after their hair, make up, and wardrobe had changed of course. Surrendering glasses for contacts was portrayed in each film as the ladder to success.

- Have you seen this "If you, then you" lie in our culture? Where?

- What are some other lies you see being fed to people in our culture?

- When God created us, He said, "It is very good." Do you struggle to feel "good"? If so, why do you think that is?

Let's go back to **Genesis 3:1-7** and focus in on verse 6: *"...and she also gave some to her husband **who was with her**."* Did you catch that? Adam was there. He was with her and yet, he said nothing.

In my early teenage years, I cared for a boy much older than I was. We talked of "love" like we knew what it was and wrote letters to one another daily. I was hooked – line and sinker. I hung on every word he said and worshipped the ground he walked on. The relationship was unhealthy, dangerous, and in the end, left me broken.

I look back and wish that my friends had spoke up. I wish they had told me that this wasn't meant to last. I wish they would have reminded me about what really mattered and pointed me back to Jesus.

My mom did. I hated her for it then, but now I love her for it. She called me out on my unhealthy obsession and need for his praise. She reminded me of promises I had made to the Lord about waiting on His timing.

She asked me, "Is God okay with this?"

And then when I didn't listen and got really hurt, she picked up my pieces.

Ephesians 4:15 says that love speaks the truth. It doesn't remain silent. It doesn't watch your life fall apart and do nothing. In a world full of voices telling us, "If you...then you...," love stands up and says, "That's not what God says! You are loved. You are good. You are His child."

Let's read **1 Thessalonians 5:11** together:
"Therefore encourage one another and build one another up, just as you are doing."

In Thessalonians, the word "build" not only means to "build a house," it also means to "repair." We can not only be used by God to speak against the lies of the enemy, but also to build each other up and to repair the damage that was been done by others in the past. What an incredible privilege!

- Do you have a person in your life that leaves you feeling "built up" and encouraged?

- Have you ever felt God healing your heart after a conversation with someone who spoke directly to your pain and brought comfort?

Look up **Ephesians 4:29** and write it here:

Our words should be weapons against the enemies lies – reminding those we love that they are who God says they are. Time with us should leave others feeling built up not torn down. That is why it matters not just that we speak the truth, but that we do it in love.

Read the words of **James 1:19-20** out loud:
"Know this, my beloved brothers: let every person be quick to hear, slow to speak, slow to anger; for the anger of man does not produce the righteousness of God."

- What should we be quick to do?

- **Proverbs 12:18** says that our "rash" words are like sword thrusts. Have you found that when you respond without listening, you cause others pain? Have you ever been hurt by someone's hasty and thoughtless words?

- Write about it here:

- Why do you think that listening is the first thing we are asked to do?

- How do you think listening would help us to respond more often with love?

Look up the following scriptures and unlock the truth about your tongue and the power it holds! Write a summary of the scripture below the reference.

Proverbs 18:21

Proverbs 12:18

Proverbs 15:4

Proverbs 16:28

Proverbs 17:9

Proverbs 12:13-14

Our words can heal and build up, but they also cause great damage. Knowing when to speak and how to say it matters. Slowing down to listen before we respond matters. It's truth spoken in love that bears fruit, not truth spoken in anger.

Let's read go back to **Genesis 3** and focus in on **verses 6-13**.
⁶"So when the woman saw that the tree was good for food, and that it was a delight to the eyes, and that the tree was to be desired to make one wise, she took of its fruit and ate, and she also gave some to her husband who was with her, and he ate. ⁷ Then the eyes of both were opened, and they knew that they were naked. And they sewed fig leaves together and made themselves loincloths. ⁸ And they heard the sound of the Lord God walking in the garden in the cool of the day, and the man and his wife hid themselves from the presence of

the Lord God among the trees of the garden. ⁹ But the Lord God called to the man and said to him, "Where are you?" ¹⁰ And he said, "I heard the sound of you in the garden, and I was afraid, because I was naked, and I hid myself." ¹¹ He said, "Who told you that you were naked? Have you eaten of the tree of which I commanded you not to eat?" ¹² The man said, "The woman whom you gave to be with me, she gave me fruit of the tree, and I ate." ¹³ Then the Lord God said to the woman, "What is this that you have done?" The woman said, "The serpent deceived me, and I ate."

Adam and Eve made choices that led to fear and shame.
Never before had these emotions been felt by humanity. Never before had they felt the need to hide from Father God. Take a minute and imagine the thoughts that must have been going through their minds as they heard His voice calling their names. How could they tell him what they had done? How could they face Him after the choices they had made?

- When you do something wrong, is it hard for you to admit it? Why or why not?

- When someone tells you that you did something that hurt them, how do you respond?

- Do you struggle with shame? Do you feel anxious or fearful when you have to face someone after a wrong was done? If so, why do you think that is?

Taking responsibility for wrongs done is an incredibly important part of a Godly relationship. "I'm sorry" matters as much, if not more, as "I forgive you." Adam and Eve not only hid from Father God and the conversation they dreaded, they also blamed others for their choices.

- Think back to the last time you were hurt in a relationship or you hurt someone else. How did you respond to that situation? Do you feel you handled things well? Are there things you feel you could have done differently? Write your response below:

- Have you ever been hurt by someone and had them blame someone or something else for the choices they made? How did that make you feel?

- Why do you think blaming others is so often the response we take when we do something wrong?

Proverbs 28:13 says, *"Whoever conceals his transgressions will not prosper, but he who confesses and forsakes them will obtain mercy."*

Blaming, hiding – none of this stopped Adam and Eve from having to face the consequences of their choices.

In **2 Samuel 12**, when David is confronted about his sin with Bathsheba, his response is entirely different from Adam and Eve's. David ached for what his sin had done to his relationship with God. His prayer afterward is not, "God, help me not to do bad things anymore." Instead it's, *"Create in me a clean* **heart** (Psalm 51)." Why? Because David knew that this was really an issue of the heart and any hope He had of restoration would begin with committing His heart to a pursuit of God again.

Confrontation can reveal a great deal about what is in us.
Luke 6:45 says that "*out of the heart, the mouth speaks.*" What "boils" over when the heat is on? How do you respond to critiques, corrections, and hard conversations? A smart defense? Denial? Anger? Blame? Your response can reveal a great deal about what is in your heart. It can also reveal a great deal about what you value most in this life.

Years ago, I found myself discouraged and upset over a situation involving a person I dearly loved. As I stood in front of them letting them know clearly how I felt about their behavior and how they could best turn things around, I heard the voice of the Father ever so gently remind me of the words of **Proverbs 10:19:** *"In the abundance of words, sin abounds."* Ouch.

When I finally stopped talking and listened, I realized that their actions had been fueled by hurt over something that I had done. Owning that and repenting was the first step in restoring what had been broken. Next came an honest dialogue about how we handled the situation and how we could do it differently in the future. We both grew – so did our relationship – from that conversation. A conversation we would have never had if I had kept talking.

Remember **James 1** encourages us to be "*slow to speak*" and "*quick to listen.*" I wonder how many offenses, wounds, and broken relationships are direct results of rash words spoken in the "heat of the moment?" And I wonder how many would be avoided if we slowed down to hear one another, humbly took responsibility for the choices we have made, and willingly had the "hard conversations" that real relationships require?

Application Questions

1. What relationships in my life need to be my focus over the next few weeks?

2. What will I do this week to intentionally invest in my relationships?

3. What is my biggest "take-a-way" from this lesson?

4. Are there people in my life I have hurt by my pride or unwillingness to say sorry? Are there people I have wounded because of the way I have presented my "truth"? Are there people I haven't been very gracious to in my life? Have I devalued people that I love with my words or actions? *Take a few moments to repent and ask God how He would like you to proceed in those relationships.*

Part 2

Leaving the Garden

Lesson 3

Genesis 4:1-16

"Now Adam knew Eve his wife, and she conceived and bore Cain, saying, "I have gotten a man with the help of the Lord." ² And again, she bore his brother Abel. Now Abel was a keeper of sheep, and Cain a worker of the ground. ³ In the course of time Cain brought to the Lord an offering of the fruit of the ground, ⁴ and Abel also brought of the firstborn of his flock and of their fat portions. And the Lord had regard for Abel and his offering, ⁵ but for Cain and his offering he had no regard. So Cain was very angry, and his face fell. ⁶ The Lord said to Cain, "Why are you angry, and why has your face fallen? ⁷ If you do well, will you not be accepted? And if you do not do well, sin is crouching at the door. Its desire is contrary to you, but you must rule over it."

⁸ Cain spoke to Abel his brother. And when they were in the field, Cain rose up against his brother Abel and killed him. ⁹ Then the Lord said to Cain, "Where is Abel your brother?" He said, "I do not know; am I my brother's keeper?" ¹⁰ And the Lord said, "What have you done? The voice of your brother's blood is crying to me from the ground. ¹¹ And now you are cursed from the ground, which has opened its mouth to receive your brother's blood from your hand. ¹² When you work the ground, it shall no longer yield to you its strength. You shall be a fugitive and a wanderer on the earth." ¹³ Cain said to the Lord, "My punishment is greater than I can bear. ¹⁴ Behold, you have driven

me today away from the ground, and from your face I shall be hidden. I shall be a fugitive and a wanderer on the earth, and whoever finds me will kill me." [15] Then the Lord said to him, "Not so! If anyone kills Cain, vengeance shall be taken on him sevenfold." And the Lord put a mark on Cain, lest any who found him should attack him. [16] Then Cain went away from the presence of the Lord and settled in the land of Nod, east of Eden."

Hebrews 11:4 tells us that Abel's sacrifice was motivated by his faith in God. Over and over again in Scripture we see that, for God, it's not **what** we give that matters. It's **why** we give. Abel's sacrifice came from a heart that believed in God and who He said He was. Cain's did not. God knew Cain's heart was not in it. He knew that "faith" and "love" were not motivating his sacrifice. When Cain responded to God's correction and warning it was with anger.

Why wasn't his gift found pleasing?
Why was Abel God's favorite?

Ultimately, Cain's issue was with God, yet Abel was the one he targeted. Abel who said nothing to Cain. Abel who had not rejected Cain's sacrifice. Abel who had done nothing wrong.

- Why do you think Cain went after Abel instead of God?

This past year, my children and I studied volcanoes. One of our unit projects required us to build our own volcano from various materials and "explode" it with baking soda and vinegar so that we could watch the "lava" fill up the chamber within the volcano and spew out from the top. As I watched the chamber fill, I realized how much people can be like volcanoes. **The pressure of all we have "stuffed" inside and not dealt with can too often lead to "explosions" with far reaching consequences.** Cain was one such "volcano." Erupting with unresolved rage, he killed Abel and the cost of that explosion was not only his brother, but also his birthright and his family.

In **Genesis 4:13,** Cain cries, "*"My punishment is greater than I can bear."* Can't you hear his agony? Every time I read this passage of scripture, my heart breaks for Abel, for Cain, and for all that was lost. It didn't have to end this way – with a mother mourning the loss of both of her sons.

Open your Bible and read the following portions of scripture: **1 Samuel 18: 6-16** and **1 Samuel 20:30-34**.

- Who was Saul really upset with?

- Why do you think it bothered him so much that David was respected and celebrated?

- Who became the "easy target" for his anger?

- Is there anyone in your life who often becomes the "easy target" for your emotions? If so, why do you think that is?

- Is there anyone in your life that you feel use you as their "easy target" for? How does that make you feel? How do you respond?

Look up the following scriptures and write them below:

Proverbs 29:11

Proverbs 15:18

Ephesians 4:31-32 says,

"³¹ Let all bitterness and wrath and anger and clamor and slander be put away from you, along with all malice. ³² Be kind to one another, tenderhearted, forgiving one another, as God in Christ forgave you."

In this portion of scripture, Paul is defining for the church in Ephesus what the "new man" looks like. In **2 Corinthians 5:17** it says that when we come to Christ we are made a new creation and old things pass away. Paul writes in verse 31, that as "new men (and women)" in Christ Jesus, we must get rid of our bitterness, wrath, anger, clamor, evil speaking and malice. This doesn't fit us anymore.

Bitterness is defined in the Strong's Concordance as "bitter hatred" and a "bitter root that produces bitter fruit." It refuses reconciliation and poisons our hearts towards others.

Wrath is passionate anger, a fierce indignation that leads to outburst of violence, rage, and temper. Anger is defined as "emotional impulse." Anger says, "I feel it, so I do it." It doesn't think about the consequences until after the choice has been made.

Clamor is defined as "loud yelling" and evil speaking encapsulates slander, lying and any words that injure others. Bottom line: **God says we have to deal with these things.** They can't go with us. They can't stay in us.

- As you look at the list, do you see any that you struggle with?

- Do you tend to be moved by emotion when you respond to others?

- How will these things hinder us from walking in the "abundant life" that Jesus offers?

According to verse 32, taking off the things that no longer "fit" us as new creations is only the first part. The second is putting on kindness, a tender heart, and forgiveness.

Kindness is defined as "goodness, graciousness, and gentleness." This is what befits a follower of Jesus. When one possesses a tender heart, he or she is moved with compassion and feels great empathy for others. Their heart is set on reconciliation, giving grace, and releasing forgiveness even to the unrepentant. Not once does it tell us that we should do these things because others deserves it or have earned it in some way. The only reason we are given for choosing kindness, compassion, and forgiveness is that "Christ forgave us" so likewise, we should forgive others.

- Which one of these three attributes of a follower of Jesus is the most challenging for you to live out on a daily basis and why do you think that is?

The truth is, if we have any hope at all, of letting go of the things that threaten to destroy our relationships and our lives – we are going to need the help of Jesus. He is our only hope of transformation, our only hope of learning to walk in kindness, compassion, and forgiveness.

Romans 12:1-2

"I appeal to you therefore, brothers, by the mercies of God, to present your bodies as a living sacrifice, holy and acceptable to God, which is your spiritual worship. 2 Do not be conformed to this world, but be transformed by the renewal of your mind, that by testing you may discern what is the will of God, what is good and acceptable and perfect."

As we bring our lives to the Lord as "living sacrifices" and lay all that we are on the altar– His fire will refine us and remove from us all that does not belong. I can't tell you how many times I have had to lay my attitude before the Lord and ask Him to purify me, how many times I have felt the volcano about to erupt and found a quiet room to get real with Jesus and pour out my heart before Him before I exploded. The transformation has always began in the place of surrender and continued with the choice to "renew my mind."

This happens through the *"washing with water by the Word* (**Ephesians 5:26**)." As we open our Bibles and dig into scripture, as we study out the truths of His Word, and as we memorize and meditate on the verses we read – the chamber of heart will fill to overflowing. Yet this time, the outpour will not bring damage. It will bring healing.

Fill in the blanks of **Galatians 5:22-23** to uncover what the result will be when we "fill up" the chamber of our heart with the RIGHT things…

"²² But the fruit of the Spirit is _____, _____,

_____,

_____, _____,

_____, _____,

²³ _____, _____; against such things there is no law."

- What are some things that have helped you let go of anger, frustration or stress that is bottled up inside? What has helped you heal from hurt caused by others?

- Are you good at "letting go" or do you tend to hold on to things for a long time? If so, why do you think that is?

- Which type of "explosion" is the most common in your life – one that brings damage or one that brings healing?

Open your Bible to **Matthew 26: 47-56** and highlight the portions of this story that stand out to you as you read.

- What emotions do you think Jesus was feeling in the Garden?

- Do you think his emotions were a valid response to what was happening?

- What does Jesus do with His emotions?

- How many times does He go back and pray?

In this portion of Scripture, Jesus gives us such a beautiful example to follow. Here we see Jesus:

1. **Take what He feels to the Father.**
2. **Lay down what He wants for what God wants.**
3. **Continue in the place of prayer until He is finished.**

- When you continue on in the story, how does Jesus' demeanor change? How does He respond when they come to take Him away?

- How does Peter respond?

- How does Jesus respond to Peter's outburst?

I love that Jesus goes back to prayer again and again and again. I love that each time He returns to the place of prayer, it is to pray the exact same prayer over and over. It reminds me to keep coming to God with my hurt, frustration, bitterness, and anger. It encourages me to continue praying until I can leave that place of prayer with my heart matching His own. It challenges me to face head on the areas in my heart that are not surrendered to His will and present my life as a "living sacrifice."

Too many believers are losing their witness because of outbursts of emotion. Too many marriages, families, and friendships are being destroyed by people stuffed so full of unresolved issues they overflow unto easy targets. People of God, hear me. This is not who we are to be. Present yourself today as a "living sacrifice." Let God's Word transform you from the inside out. You won't regret it.

James 1:20

"For the anger of man does not produce the righteousness of God."

Application Questions

1. What relationships in my life need to be my focus over the next few weeks?

2. What is my biggest "take-a-way" from this lesson?

3. What are the emotions that often overwhelm me and begin to affect my response towards others? What is a healthy way for me to deal with these emotions when they arise?

4. Are there people in my life I have yet to release forgiveness too? Why? What do I need to do to move forward in this?

Lesson 4

As we continue our journey beyond the Garden, we come to the story of Noah. Noah was a faithful man in a faithless world. **Genesis 6:5** says, *"⁵ The LORD saw that the wickedness of man was great in the earth, and that every intention of the thoughts of his heart was only evil continually,"* but goes on to say in **verse 8**, *"But Noah found favor in the eyes of the Lord."*

Hebrews 11:6 tells us that:

"⁷ By faith Noah, being warned by God concerning events as yet unseen, in reverent fear constructed an ark for the saving of his household. By this he condemned the world and became an heir of the righteousness that comes by faith."

- What does this portion of scripture tell us motivated Noah's obedience?

- What do you think "reverent fear" is?

Take a moment to open your Bible and read **Genesis 6 & 7** from beginning to end. Imagine that you are Noah for a moment. No one else is building an Ark. No one else is preparing for rain.

- How would you feel? What thoughts would be going through your head?

- Would it be hard to obey God when no one else was? Why or why not?

- Have you ever had a time in your life when you felt like the only one trying to do the right thing? Write about it here:

"Noah and the Ark" is so much more than a children's book full of adorable animals and simple songs. It is so much more than a story about a boat. This story holds within it so many lessons that apply to us today. One important one being this: **keep doing the right thing even if no one else does.**

In our lives, there will be times when others break promises, hurt our feelings, and say the wrong thing out of anger. Husbands will look past the new haircut and forget anniversaries. Wives will question choices being made and make their husbands feel disrespected. Children will scream out their frustrations. Friends will not always be available when we need them. What will we do then? Who will we be in those spaces? Will we still be faithful? Will we still do the right thing even if we are the only one?

In the end, Noah's faithfulness led to his family's salvation. When the doors opened and they placed their feet on dry land once again; when he looked at his wife and children safe and alive – you can bet that Noah had no regrets.

Genesis 8 concludes at an altar. Noah worships God and God responds with a promise to never again flood the entire earth. A covenant is made by a covenant-keeping God, a covenant that has been kept generation after generation. Why? Because God is faithful. He is always faithful. No matter what.

Genesis 9:20-27

*"**20** Noah began to be a man of the soil, and he planted a vineyard. **21** He drank of the wine and became drunk and lay uncovered in his tent. **22** And Ham, the father of Canaan, saw the nakedness of his father and told his two brothers outside. **23** Then Shem and Japheth took a garment, laid it on both their shoulders, and walked backward and covered the nakedness of their father. Their faces were turned backward, and they did not see their father's nakedness. **24** When Noah awoke from his wine and knew what his youngest son had done to him, **25** he said, "Cursed be Canaan; ʲa servant of servants shall he be to his brothers." **26** He also said, "Blessed be the Lord, the God of Shem; and let Canaan be his servant. **27** May God enlarge Japheth, and let him dwell in the tents of Shem, and let Canaan be his servant."*

- What did Ham do when he saw his father's nakedness?

- What did the other brothers do?

- How might this story apply to your relationships?

Shem and Japheth covered over the their father's nakedness. They walked backwards into the tent so that when he was coherent he would not be embarrassed. They refused to shame him. They chose honor even when Noah's behavior was less than honorable. It led to a blessing. And in this, we learn another important lesson: **how we treat others when they make a mistake matters.**

Ham not only shamed his father by entering the tent and watching him make a spectacle of himself, but he also went and told others about it. So many of believer's share gossip under the disguise of a "prayer request." We whisper complaints about our spouses to our friends over the phone or over lunch in the breakroom, but when was the last time we actually prayed for our spouses? So many women sit around coffee shop tables and "spill the tea" about Sally at the office and Jane on the worship team, yet when was the last time "Sally at the office" was on our prayer list? When was the last time we invited her to coffee? Checked in on her? Invited her to lunch?

Or how about the new guy at work that just doesn't seem to be getting it and is slowing down production? Men – instead of getting angry and complaining, have you tried to invite him to lunch? Tried to reach out? Spoke a word of encouragement?

- How do you respond to people when they are going through a hard time? Do you walk away? Do you talk about them? Or do you do something to help?

- Are you a gossip? Do you join in when others are gossiping?

- Think of people in your life that are going through a hard time or making decisions that you know are unhealthy for them. When is the last time you prayed for them?

Look up the following portions of scripture and write a short summary of the verse below it:

Proverbs 11:13

Proverbs 16:28

Proverbs 17:9

Proverbs 20:19

Proverbs 26:20

Gossip destroys relationships. In **Psalm 141 verse 3**, the Psalmist prays, *"Set a guard, O Lord, over my mouth; keep watch over the door of my lips!"* Let this also be our prayer.

James 3 verse 5 reminds us that *"the tongue is a small member, yet it boasts of great things."* A wise woman knows the power of her words and learns to use them in a way that glorifies the Lord and speaks life into those around her.

Genesis 11:1-9

"Now the whole earth had one language and the same words. ² And as people migrated from the east, they found a plain in the land of Shinar and settled there. ³ And they said to one another, "Come, let us make bricks, and burn them thoroughly." And they had brick for stone, and bitumen for mortar. ⁴ Then they said, "Come, let us build ourselves a city and a tower with its top in the heavens, and let us make a name for ourselves, lest we be dispersed over the face of the whole earth." ⁵ And the Lord came down to see the city and the tower, which the children of man had built. ⁶ And the Lord said, "Behold, they are one people, and they have all one language, and this is only the beginning of what they will do. And nothing that they propose to do will now be impossible for them. ⁷ Come, let us go down and there confuse their language, so that they may not understand one another's speech." ⁸ So the Lord dispersed them from there over the face of all the earth, and they left off building the city. ⁹ Therefore its name was called Babel, because there the Lord confused the language of all the earth. And from there the Lord dispersed them over the face of all the earth."

- Why do you think God wanted to "stop" the building of the tower?

- When God wanted to "stop" the building of the tower, what did He do?

The people had banded together and remained close after the flood. As their numbers grew, so did their pride. In **Genesis 1-2**, God had been clear that mankind was to *"fill the earth and subdue it."* Instead, they built a tower to house them all in one place. No one left. No one spread out. No one obeyed. God had to act.

Mixing up their languages stopped the building of the tower and made living together in one place virtually impossible. Once they couldn't communicate, they couldn't work together. Spreading out was the only option to have any form of peace on earth. If you can't understand each other, you can't live together. Isn't that how it still is?

Over half of all marriages end in divorce because of poor communication. Our inability to communicate properly has led to explosive conflicts, negativity, cold and callous hearts towards others, employee frustration, confusion, and distrust. It is the cause behind hurt feelings, misunderstanding, and almost all arguments. Search "communication" on the internet and thousands of articles will appear. Everyone wants to know how to communicate better. Everyone is searching for the secret to the best communication styles. Why? Because everybody knows: **relationships don't work if you can't communicate.**

Acts 2:1-8

"When the day of Pentecost arrived, they were all together in one place. ² And suddenly there came from heaven a sound like a mighty rushing wind, and it filled the entire house where they were sitting. ³ And divided tongues as of fire appeared to them and rested on each one of them. ⁴ And they were all filled with the Holy Spirit and began to speak in other tongues as the Spirit gave them utterance.

⁵ Now there were dwelling in Jerusalem Jews, devout men from every nation under heaven. ⁶ And at this sound the multitude came together, and they were bewildered, because each one was hearing them speak in his own language. ⁷ And they were amazed and astonished, saying, "Are not all these who are speaking Galileans? ⁸ And how is it that we hear, each of us in his own native language?"

- After the outpouring of the Holy Spirit, what happened?

- Even though the disciples spoke in Hebrew, everyone heard them in what? (Verse 8)

The God who had "confused" languages in Genesis was now bringing "clarity" to communication and supernaturally helping everyone to hear one another in the language that they would understand! This is crucial for us to grab ahold of. We must never minimize the gift of the Holy Spirit when it comes to establishing good communication in our relationships. He can supernaturally bring clarity where there is confusion, wisdom where it is lacking (**James 1**), and revelation where there needs to be revelation (**Ephesians 1**).

Ask the Lord to help you the next time you face a communication problem in your relationships. Choose to be "*slow to speak*" and "*quick to listen*" – not just to the other person and what they are communicating, but to the Holy Spirit and what He is sharing with you.

Proverbs 3:5-6

"Trust in the Lord with all your heart,
and do not lean on your own understanding.
⁶ In all your ways acknowledge him,
and he will make straight your paths."

Good communication may not be the easiest thing to establish in your relationships, but it is worth investing in. It's worth taking the time to slow down and listen. It's worth learning to let the

Holy Spirit lead. Just ask the people of Babel. Relationships don't work if we can't communicate.

Some Last Tips When It Comes To Communication:
1. Avoid name calling and unkind words.
2. Value the feelings of others – even if you don't agree with them.
3. Use a calm, respectful tone.
4. Confirm your love for the person.
5. Stay on topic and avoid ultimatums like, "If you treat me like that again, I'm done with you." As a married couple, treat the word "divorce" like the plague.

Application Questions

1. What is the biggest communication mistake that I make in my relationships?

2. What is one way that I have been hurt in the past by poor communication?

3. How have I handled confrontation in the past? Has it been effective?

4. Do I find it difficult to have the hard conversations? Why?

Part 3
Beyond the Garden

Lesson 5

Genesis 12-50 continues on with the story of one family – the family of Abraham - that would later take on the name "Israel." The story is filled with victories, defeats, struggles, and joys. We see the effects of favoritism, deception, unchecked emotions, bitterness, and abuse. We see relationships destroyed by choices to react in anger and relationships healed by the choice to forgive. Lessons are everywhere, written upon every line of their story. Some of the lessons are written on the mountain tops of triumph and some are carved out in deep valleys of pain. It is one of these valleys we meet Rachel and Leah.

Open your Bible and read **Genesis 29:1-30** as we begin.

- What was the name of the woman that Jacob loved?

- How is she described in this portion of scripture?

- Who is the woman Jacob is deceived into marrying?

- How is she described in this portion of scripture?

- How does Jacob respond to Laban's deception?

From the start Leah is aware, "Jacob never wanted me." Women, can you imagine knowing that the rest of your life will be spent with a man who only married you because your father tricked him? Translate that to your lives, Men. Can you imagine spending the rest of your life married to a woman how was forced to marry but had no feelings for you? Their marriage is loveless, lonely, and void of any real connection from the start. Jacob's heart – as it had been from the beginning – was Rachels. She was the one he wanted.

With this in mind, it's no surprise that sorrow finds a home in the heart of Leah.

Genesis 29:31-35

"When the Lord saw that Leah was hated, he opened her womb, but Rachel was barren. ³² And Leah conceived and bore a son, and she called his name Reuben, for she said, "Because the Lord has looked upon my affliction; for now my husband will love me." ³³ She

conceived again and bore a son, and said, "Because the Lord has heard that I am hated, he has given me this son also." And she called his name Simeon. ³⁴ Again she conceived and bore a son, and said, "Now this time my husband will be attached to me, because I have borne him three sons." Therefore his name was called Levi. ³⁵ And she conceived again and bore a son, and said, "This time I will praise the Lord." Therefore she called his name Judah. Then she ceased bearing.

- As you look at the names Leah gave her sons and the meanings behind them, what does it make you feel for Leah? Why?

- What do the meanings of her son's names show us she really wanted?

With each child that she births for Jacob, Leah hopes, "Maybe now my husband will love me." But he doesn't. **Leah knew pain.** She knew what it felt like to be unwanted, unseen, and unloved.

Continue reading in **Genesis 30:1-24.**

- What does Rachel cry out to God in verse 1?

- Why do you think she said this to God?

As Rachel watched how Jacob interacted with Leah's sons, jealousy found a home in her heart. In a culture where birthing sons was the greatest honor and highest privilege of a woman – Rachel felt like a failure. As Leah's sons ran through the camp and threw themselves on Jacob's lap, Rachel's womb ached with bareness.

- Have you ever felt jealous when things you have wanted for a long time happen to someone else? How did you/do you handle it?

- How can jealousy hinder and hurt a relationship?

- What fueled Rachel's jealousy?

Like Leah, **Rachel knew pain**. She knew what it felt like to feel like a worthless, to feel broken, and to carry shame. **Both sisters were hurting.** Neither of them could see past their own pain and because of it, they caused pain for one another. There are a lot of lessons here for us.

- Can you think of some? Write them below:

Sometimes we can get so wrapped up in our own lives, we forget to look up – to see people. We forget that everyone has a story.

1 Samuel 1:1-6

"There was a certain man of Ramathaim-zophim of the hill country of Ephraim whose name was Elkanah the son of Jeroham, son of Elihu, son of Tohu, son of Zuph, an Ephrathite. ² He had two wives. The name of the one was Hannah, and the name of the other, Peninnah. And Peninnah had children, but Hannah had no children. ³ Now this man used to go up year by year from his city to worship and to sacrifice to the Lord of hosts at Shiloh, where the two sons of Eli, Hophni and Phinehas, were priests of the Lord. ⁴ On the day when Elkanah sacrificed, he would give portions to Peninnah his wife and to all her sons and daughters. ⁵ But to Hannah he gave a double portion, because he loved her, though the Lord had closed her womb. ⁶ And her rival used to provoke her grievously to irritate her, because the Lord had closed her womb."

- Often when we read this story, we focus on Hannah. This time, I want us to focus on Peninnah. Why do you think Peninnah provoked Hannah? Was it about more than her closed womb?

Now, let's go to the story of Joseph and his brothers in **Genesis 37:1-4:**

> *"Jacob lived in the land of his father's sojournings, in the land of Canaan.*
> *² These are the generations of Jacob. Joseph, being seventeen years old, was pasturing the flock with his brothers. He was a boy with the sons of Bilhah and Zilpah, his father's wives. And Joseph brought a bad report of them to their father. ³ Now Israel loved Joseph more than any other of his sons, because he was the son of his old age. And he made him a robe of many colors. ⁴ But when his brothers saw that their father loved him more than all his brothers, they hated him and could not speak peacefully to him."*

- As you read this portion of scripture, do you see why Joseph's brothers may have been so unkind to Joseph?

So often when we read the story of Hannah, we paint Peninnah as a villain. *Who would mock a woman who is going through such heartbreak?* The answer is a woman who longs to be loved as deeply by her husband; a woman insecure about her position in the family; a woman who has provided her husband with sons to carry on his name and yet still watches as he gives another woman the double portion.

And what of Joseph's brothers? Sons of the unwanted wife. Born of duty not love. From the day of their birth they have known: "We shouldn't be here. He didn't want this." What of their pain? The pain of watching their beloved mother spend her life wooing a man in love with someone else. The pain of watching the sister's cruel responses to one another year after year. And what about the pain of having a father who tossed them to the side the moment his dear Rachel gave birth to the "wanted" son? Too often, we ignore this side of the story and in doing so, we lose a lesson that we must learn. **Ours is not the only story**.

More often than not, there is reason why people respond the way they do. There is a reason a spouse recoils to touch, a child refuses to honor a parent, and a friendship turns cold. It is so much bigger than your story. Your spouse, child, and friend have one too. If only you will listen.

1 Corinthians 10:24 reminds us that no one should seek their own good, but seek "the good of his neighbor." In **John 4:35**, when Jesus is telling His disciples that the fields are ready to be harvested, He tells them first to "look up" and see the harvest. It was ready – heavy with grain - but they couldn't see until they looked up.

Too often, we can get so consumed in our own lives we stop looking up. Technology has only made it worse. Entire meals will be eaten around the dinner table with no conversation. The only sound in the room is the buzz and beep of incoming text messages. Real, live conversation has too often been replaced by a dozen tweets and retweets. We assume we know somebody because we follow them on Instagram. Genuine conversation has been sidelined for short exchanges over the internet. And not only that, we live in a world full of distractions. Deadlines. Due Dates. Noise. Entertainment. Schedules. Responsibilities. All of it takes our eyes off of the person in front of us. Yet in the midst of all it, people are crying out to be seen – for somebody to look up and take notice.

- When is the last time you asked your friend how they are doing?

- When was the last unhurried conversation you had with your spouse? Child? Friend? Sibling?

- The last time you had a disagreement in your relationship and walked away hurt – how did you resolve it? Did you take time to hear the other person's story?

- Why do you think it can be so difficult for us to see past our own pain and our own story?

- What do you think Rachel and Leah could have done to change the outcome of their story?

Philippians 2:1-8 has been one of my favorite portions of scripture for as long as I can remember. As we end this lesson, I want you to read through the verse slowly. Highlight key words and phrases that stand out to you as read.

"So if there is any encouragement in Christ, any comfort from love, any participation in the Spirit, any affection and sympathy, ² complete my joy by being of the same mind, having the same love, being in full accord and of one mind. ³ Do nothing from selfish ambition or conceit, but in humility count others more significant than yourselves. ⁴ Let each of you look not only to his own interests, but also to the interests of others. ⁵ Have this mind among yourselves, which is yours in Christ Jesus, ⁶ who, though he was in the form of God, did not count equality with God a thing to be grasped, ⁷ but emptied himself, by taking the form of a servant, being born in the likeness of men. ⁸ And being found in human form, he humbled himself by becoming obedient to the point of death, even death on a cross."

- What would have happened if Rachel and Leah had lived out this scripture? How do you think the story could have been changed?

- How could this attitude that was in Christ have changed the story of Hannah and Peninnah?

- How could it have changed the story of Joseph and his brothers?

In **Matthew 12 verses 30 through 31**, Jesus tells us that the first commandment is to simply *"Love the Lord your God with all your heart and with all your soul and with all your mind and with all your strength' and the second is to 'Love your neighbor as yourself.'* He goes on to say that *"No other commandment is greater than these."*

When the rich young ruler asks Jesus who his neighbor is in **Luke 10**, Jesus tells him the story of a Jewish man who cares for a wounded man of Samaria. He tells this story during a time in history when the Jewish people and the Samaritans were not on good terms. They refused to even drink from the same cup or share the same bowl (**John 4:9**). Through the telling of this story Jesus answered the rich young ruler's question.

Your neighbor is: **anybody**. It's the person next to you. It's your cashier at Wal Mart. It's the single mom trying to hold her baby and get her groceries in her car. It's the co-worker who sits alone at break time. And it's the woman who treats you like the joke of the office, the kid who never thanks you for all you do, and the husband who falls asleep on date night. It's all of them – and you aren't called to fix them. You are called to love them.

So, now the question is, "H*ow do you love your neighbor as yourself?"*

The answer is found in this simple statement: **what you do for yourself, you should do for others.**

Do you make sure you eat? *Make sure they eat too.*

Do you make sure your needs are met? *Meet their needs too.*

Do you pick your favorite movie to watch at night? *Let them pick too.*

Look up and see the people around you. Get to know them. Love them. Take the time to hear their story. Seek their good not just your own. Silence the cell phone. Have real conversation. Ask people how they are doing. Don't just assume you know. Slow down. Look Up. Don't miss them. God placed these people in your life. There is so much waiting for us on the other side of looking up.

Application Questions

1. What is my biggest take-a-way from this lesson?

2. Who are some people in my life that it is hard for me to "see past" their actions to the "pain" that might be behind them? Why do I think that is?

3. Do I think I take time to really see the people in my life? If not, why not? What distracts me? If yes, how?

4. What is one intentional thing I can do this week to "seek the good" of my neighbor?

Lesson 6

The book of Genesis ends with the story of Joseph, one of the twelve sons of Israel and great-grandson of Abraham. Born to a mother who had spent years crying out for a child of her own, his birth was met with great joy. He was a miracle – a child of her old age and an answer to her prayers.

Yet from the moment he arrived, his brothers despised him. Joseph was the "wanted" son of the "wanted" wife. They were the sons of a marriage that should have never happened. They shouldn't have been there They wouldn't been there if not for a grandfather who deceived their father into marrying their mother.

As the years went by and Joseph grew, so did the love that his father, Jacob, had for him. A coat of many colors was made for him and placed upon his shoulders – a sign of his father's love. No other son received such a gift. Overtime, jealousy became hatred and we witness a family broken by favoritism, pride, anger, and sin.

Let's begin reading in **Genesis 37:12-36.**

- As you read this portion of scripture, is there a part of you that says the brother's were justified in what they did? Why or why not?

- Why did they do it?

- Have you ever "got even" with someone else or wanted to?

- How did you feel afterwards?

- How do you think Joseph felt as he was led away to Egypt?

- Now put yourself in the place of Jacob. What emotions do you think he felt when he heard the news of his son's death?

- As they watched their father mourn, do you think the brother's regretted what they done? Why or why not?

Genesis 37 always brings me to tears. I ache for the father who lost his beloved child, for the sons who simply wanted to be loved by their father, and for the boy abused by his own flesh and blood. I read this story and I think, "How did this happen?" And then...I think of puzzles.

I hate puzzles, but I also love them. There is nothing like the joy found in completing something that has challenged you and made you question your intellect. There is also nothing like the frustration found in holding a piece they say fits into the puzzle but it doesn't. My oldest son use to spend hours leaning over a puzzle studying the pieces intently.

My son, Daniel, on the other hand, would just sit waiting for "the moment" - the moment he would be released like a bull rushing from the bull pen, to break the puzzle apart once again. This was and is his favorite part of puzzle-building. Demolition Daniel! What took days, even weeks, to build is completely destroyed within minutes. Our relationships can be destroyed just as quickly. One word, one choice is all that it takes.

- Have you ever had a relationship in your life that felt "unfixable?" Write about it here:

- Are there relationships in your life that you have given up because they seem too broken?

It is rare that my children ever rebuild after Demolition Daniel gets his hands on the puzzle we built. Why? Because they know what took him seconds to destroy could take hours, even days to rebuild. And who wants to do that all over again? **Who wants to take the time?**

Who wants to sit through the awkward silence that comes when two friends that have hurt each other don't know what to say?

Who wants to try to win the heart of their spouse again – walking over the shards of glass to woo one that once seemed strong and now is so "fragile?"

Who wants to have to admit they were wrong?

Who wants to say sorry?

Genesis 42 opens with a great famine covering the land. By this point, Joseph has made his way to the palace and is now second in command of Egypt. Because of the Pharaoh's dream and Joseph's interpretation, Egypt sits poised to not only survive the famine but also help neighboring countries survive as well. But when Joseph's brothers arrive in Egypt asking for grain, Joseph finds himself face to face with his abusers and with an important choice to make. Will he give them a second chance?

Take some time to read **Genesis 43, 44, and 45**. Note the way Joseph treats his brothers and how his brothers respond.

- How many times does it say that Joseph wept? Why do you think he felt so overwhelmed with emotion?

- What do the brother's say and do that expresses their regret over what they have done?

- How does Joseph say God used what his brother's did to him for good?

Over the years, I have learned that **restoration takes time and patience.** Like a broken puzzle, the pieces of our shattered hearts must be put back together piece by piece. This is not always an easy process. Trust must be built. Communication must be re-established. Often what took seconds to destroy will take much longer to rebuild.

I remember reading an article in a magazine years ago in which an elderly couple who had been married for over sixty five years was asked the secret to a long and happy marriage.

"We lived in a time," they responded, " where when something was broken, you fixed it. You didn't throw it away."

Galatians 6:9 promises that we will reap a harvest if we do not give up. Women of God, I can promise you, there will be days you want to give up and people you want to give up on. There will be days where "trashing" it sounds a whole lot better than "fixing" what has been broken. But if we do, we will miss the harvest.

- Do you think you could have forgiven Joseph's brother's after all they done wrong? Why or why not?

- What do you think they felt when Joseph released forgiveness to them?

Joseph's forgiveness was fueled by his ability to see God at work in the midst of all that had happened to him. He would go on to comfort his brother's after their father's death in **Genesis 50** with these words: *"Do not fear, for am I in the place of*

God? ²⁰ As for you, you meant evil against me, but God meant it for good, to bring it about that many people should be kept alive, as they are today. ²¹ So do not fear; I will provide for you and your little ones (verses 19-21)."

This is an important key to restoration. **We have to gain a "God-Perspective."** Joseph could see all the good God had done through His pain. He could see His brothers through the eyes of a loving God.

Isaiah 55:8-9 says…

*"For my thoughts are not your thoughts,
neither are your ways my ways, declares the LORD.
⁹ For as the heavens are higher than the earth,
so are my ways higher than your ways
and my thoughts than your thoughts."*

I like to think of life as a giant chess board. I am a pawn with only a short-sighted view of the board, but God is the one above it all who sees why each move must happen in the way that it does. He sees the whole picture. He knows the outcome. So often my anger towards someone has completely disappeared simply by gaining a God-perspective. Discouragement has been replaced with hope when I have been able to see how God is working all things together for my good (Romans 8). Bottom line: **if we have any hope of restoration for our broken**

relationships – it will begin and end on our knees in the place of prayer. We must ask God to help us to forgive those who have hurt us and *"open the eyes of our understanding"* to see what He sees (Ephesians 1). This is where restoration begins.

- What are the most amazing parts of this story for you?

- What are some of the biggest lessons you see within this story?

- Which is your biggest struggle: having patience, truly forgiving, or seeing it all from God's perspective? Why?

Grace is getting what we don't deserve. Grace is how God responds to our failures and how God calls us to respond towards those who fail us. Grace is what Joseph offered his brothers and what we are asked to give even to the undeserving.

Romans 5:6-8 says:
"For while we were still weak, at the right time, Christ died for the ungodly. For one will scarcely die for a righteous person – though perhaps for a good person one would dare to even die – but God shows His love for us in that while we were still sinners, Christ died for us. "

And **Ephesians 2:4** tell us:
"But God being rich in mercy, because of His great love with which He has loved us, even when we were dead in our trespasses, made us alive together with Christ – by grace you have been saved…"

In a world that says, "Pay them back," be the person who refuses to.
In a society that tells us, "Get even," be the person who forgives.
In a generation that shouts, "Earn my respect," be the one who outdoes everyone in showing honor (Romans 12:10).
Walk in grace.

Choose restoration.

Do the work of rebuilding.

The Bible says that "while we were yet sinners, Christ died for us." While we were YET sinners – lost in our mess, our brokenness, our mistakes – when we didn't return it and we definitely hadn't earned it; He died for us. This is the heart of our Father and this is at the very core of how we should love one another.

Application Questions

1. What is my biggest take-a-way from this lesson?

2. Are there relationships in my life that need to be rebuilt? When is the last time I prayed about those relationships? When is the last time I asked God to give me His perspective and help me to forgive?

3. Are there people in my life that I need to ask for forgiveness from? Are there choices that I have made or that I am making that are effecting my relationships in a negative way? Explain:

As you end this Bible Study, I pray you walk away with lessons that will help you to continue to grow in your relationships with God and others. We are praying for you!

If you enjoyed this Bible Study, you might also enjoy:

- They Call Me Mama: *What Happens When We Say Yes To God*, by Nicole Homan (Available now on Amazon!)
- Planted Bible Study Series, Book 2: *Emotional Stability*, by Nicole Homan
- Planted Bible Study Series, Book 3: *Wisdom*, by Nicole Homan
- To Know Him As Father, by Nicole Homan

Resources Used:

English Standard Version Bible. (2001). ESV Online.
https://esv.literalword.com/

Strong's Exhaustive Concordance: New American Standard Bible. 1995. Updated ed. La Habra: Lockman Foundation.
http://www.biblestudytools.com/concordances/strongs-exhaustive-concordance/.

Made in the USA
Monee, IL
14 September 2022

12958916R00056